AFRA
Brother of Light

GREEN INTEGER
Pataphysics and Pedantry

Douglas Messerli, *Publisher*

Essays, Manifestos, Statements, Speeches, Maxims,
Epistles, Diaristic Notes, Narratives, Natural Histories,
Poems, Plays, Performances, Ramblings, Revelations
and all such ephemera as may appear necessary
to bring society into a slight tremolo of confusion
and fright at least.

*

MASTERWORKS OF FICTION
Green Integer Books

Masterworks of Fiction is a program of Green Integer
to reprint important works of fiction from all centuries.
We make no claim to any superiority of these fictions
over others in either form or subject, but rather we contend
that these works are highly enjoyable to read and,
more importantly, have challenged the ideas and language
of the times in which they were published,
establishing themselves over the years as among
the outstanding works of their period. By republishing
both well known and lesser recognized titles in this series
we hope to continue our mission bringing our society
into a slight tremolo of confusion and fright at least.

Books in this series

José Donoso *Hell Has No Limits* (1966)
Knut Hamsun *A Wanderer Plays on Muted Strings* (1909)
Raymond Federman *The Twofold Vibration* (1982)
Gertrude Stein *To Do: A Book of Alphabets and Birthdays*
(1957)
Gérard de Nerval *Aurélia* (1855)
Tereza Albues *Pedra Canga* (1987)
Sigurd Hoel *Meeting at the Milestone* (1947)
Leslie Scalapino *Defoe* (1994)
Charles Dickens *A Christmas Carol* (1843)
Michael Disend *Stomping the Goyim* (1969)

Books in the Green Integer series

History, or Messages from History Gertrude Stein [1997]
Notes on the Cinematographer Robert Bresson [1997]
The Critic As Artist Oscar Wilde [1997]
Tent Posts Henri Michaux [1997]
Eureka Edgar Allan Poe [1997]
An Interview Jean Renoir [1998]
Mirrors Marcel Cohen [1998]
The Effort to Fall Christopher Spranger [1998]
Radio Dialogs I Arno Schmidt [1999]
Travels Hans Christian Andersen [1999]
In the Mirror of the Eighth King
Christopher Middleton [1999]
On Ibsen James Joyce [1999]

Green Integer EL-E-PHANT books

BOOKS FORTHCOMING FROM GREEN INTEGER

AFRA
Brother of Light

*Spiritual Teachings
from an Ascended Master*

THE SUMMIT LIGHTHOUSE LIBRARY™

AFRA: BROTHER OF LIGHT
Teachings of Elizabeth Clare Prophet compiled by the editors
of The Summit Lighthouse Library
Copyright © 2003 The Summit Lighthouse Library
All rights reserved

For information, please contact The Summit Lighthouse Library,
PO Box 5000, Corwin Springs, MT 59030-5000.
Tel: 1-800-245-5445 or 406-848-9500.
Web site: www.summituniversitypress.com
E-mail: info@summituniversitypress.com

Library of Congress Catalog Card Number: 2002113198
ISBN: 0-9720402-8-5

THE SUMMIT LIGHTHOUSE LIBRARY™

The Summit Lighthouse Library is an imprint of Summit
University Press.

SUMMIT UNIVERSITY 🕊 PRESS

The Summit Lighthouse, Summit University Press, 🕊, Pearls of
Wisdom, Teachings of the Ascended Masters, Climb the Highest
Mountain and Science of the Spoken Word are registered trade-
marks.

Cover art, design and production: Brad Davis

Printed in the United States of America

06   05   04   03   6   5   4   3   2   1

Meet the Master

When the pupil is ready, the teacher appears.

There is a brotherhood of light—masterful beings who have graduated from earth's schoolroom. These masters are way-showers, pointing the path home to God. From the heaven realm, they assist mankind in all fields of human endeavor, helping to raise the consciousness of earth.

Each master is also a teacher in search of a student, desiring to reach from beyond the veil to touch that one for the acceleration of their spiritual evolution. The *Meet the Master* series seeks to introduce the student to the master. ❧

Meet the Master Afra

Afra—ancient patron of the continent of Africa and sponsor of the black race, comes again with a message of unity and brotherhood for his brethren everywhere. This beloved brother of light is pledged to solve the problems of divergent peoples—local wars, discord in religion, strife between Arab and Jew, between black and white, between Christian and Moslem. We need him today as never before. ✤

Table of Contents

*To the Sons and Daughters
of Afra*

SECTION I
Afra—
Brother
of Light

Who Are The
Ascended Masters?

The ascended masters are our elder brothers and sisters on the spiritual path. Having balanced their karma and fulfilled their unique mission, they have graduated from earth's schoolroom and ascended back to God in the ritual known as the ascension.

These masters are a part of a vast brother-hood of spiritual beings and angelic hosts who work with mankind for the betterment of life on earth. They are spoken of in chapter seven of the book of Revelation as the great multitude of saints "clothed with white robes" who stand before the throne of God. The white robes sig-nify the white light in the aura of the saints.*

These enlightened teachers have emerged

*The white light contains all the colors of the rainbow and does not refer to race or nationality.

from all races and nationalities and from all walks of life and all religions. Many are familiar to us, having walked among us through the ages, while others may be unknown to our outer mind. Some are ancient beings of light, unrecorded in history, and their names have long ago become secondary to the flames they bear. Whatever their origin in the vastness of our Father's universe, they all share a common light—a light they desire to share with mankind who are seeking the truth they bear.

Among these saints are Gautama Buddha, Maitreya, Jesus Christ, Saint Michael the Archangel, Zarathustra, Moses, Melchizedek, Mother Mary, Saint Francis, Saint Germain, El Morya, Kuan Yin and unnumbered and unnamed loving hearts—servants of humanity who have returned to the heart of God and are a part of the living God forevermore.

This Brotherhood works with earnest seekers and public servants of every race, religion and walk of life to assist humanity in their forward evolution. ⚜

Who Is the Master Afra?

*L*ong ago, Afra offered name and fame to God to sponsor a vast continent and a mighty people. That continent is Africa.

Afra was the first member of the black race to make his ascension. He returned to God, reuniting with the flame at the conclusion of a life of devotion and service. When he ascended, he asked to be called simply "a brother,"—or *frater* in Latin. And so "a frater" became the word *Afra*.

The continent of Africa takes its name from Afra. He is the patron of that land and also the patron of the black race. The black race, long ago, was part of what was known as the blue race and the violet race. Their skin actually had a subtle blue or violet hue. These souls lived in a spiritually advanced civilization that existed on the continent of Africa.

Africa was once a part of the continent of Lemuria—the ancient motherland, the place of culture, truth and beauty. On ancient Lemuria there was an age of freedom and enlightenment long lost to recorded history. It was a golden-age civilization with marvelous advances in science and technology.

There were, indeed, ancient golden ages in Africa, when the people came forth out of the light of the causal body of the Great Divine Director, a cosmic being who is a teacher of masters and their students. His causal body is a great blue sphere that surrounds the planet, ensouling the perfect awareness of the Father's plan for all of life. As he did in those ancient golden ages, the Great Divine Director continues to sponsor the divine plan of the continent of Africa, even as he sponsors the divine plan for the descendants of Afra in America.

Since the time of Afra's ascension, when he showed the way for all the brothers and sisters who would follow after him, many others have ascended from the black race. ⚜

16

The True Meaning of Race

From a spiritual perspective, there is no such thing as a black race or a white race. In heaven, the masters are not noted by their race or previous religion. All are known by the quality of the heart and by the flame they keep.

All of the races on earth have come forth from the heart of God under the seven rays, or seven paths of initiation. Those who are today known as the white race came forth for the mastery of the yellow (wisdom), pink (love) and white (purity) flames—hence, the various mixtures and tone qualities of their skin. These evolutions were intended to place upon the altar of God the gift of their self-mastery in the way of wisdom, love and purity.

Those of the yellow race, the people of China, serve on the ray of wisdom, while those who have red-colored skin are intended to amplify the pink flame of divine love.

The members of the black race have come forth on the blue ray and the violet ray. In the ancient civilization on the continent of Africa, the people's skin had a blue or a violet hue. These colors come from the Father-Mother God, Alpha and Omega, the beginning and the ending, the first ray and the seventh ray.

Individual nations have their own calling, or dharma. Each nation is called by God to manifest a specific virtue or fulfill a certain destiny. The members of what is now known as the black race were sent to earth to master the qualities of God's power, his will and his faith (on the blue ray) and the qualities of God's freedom, justice and mercy (on the violet ray). This continues to be their mission to this day.

Since their departure from Eden, mankind have wandered from this high estate, and the pure colors of the rainbow rays are no longer reflected either in the skin tone or in the aura. The divide-and-conquer tactics of the fallen ones have spread throughout the land. Instead of the races embracing one another as brother and sister, there is division: one race enslaves another race, and the great unity of all children of God and their oneness in the flame is destroyed. ⚜

Afra's Life on the Continent of Africa

Afra lived 500,000 years ago in an ancient civilization on the continent we now call Africa. At this time, the people of this land had reached a crossroads. Fallen angels and dark forces had invaded planet Earth and were dividing the people, setting brother against brother.

These evil angels set out to destroy the blue and the violet races. They distorted the once sacred rituals and art forms of this magnificent people. Thus, the door was opened to all manners of perversions of the light, to the practices of witchcraft, voodoo and black magic. Gradually, the dark ones turned the people toward hatred, superstition and a vying for power.

As the people began to divert their attention from their God Presence, they became more and more vulnerable to the divide-and-conquer tactics of the fallen angels. The civilization became divided by the warring factions of its tribes. And the people were losing the spiritual battle between the forces of light and darkness within them. Their division, both within and without, allowed them to become enslaved under the powers of darkness.

Seeing the plight of his people, Afra took embodiment among them in order to rescue them. First, he pinpointed the one missing trait that he perceived to be the Achilles heel of his people. He identified the point of vulnerability as their lack of brotherhood: They were following the example of Cain, rather than the example of Abel.

You will remember that the Lord looked with favor on Abel and his offering. But he looked with disfavor on Cain and his offering. As Genesis records it, Cain was very angry. "And the LORD said onto Cain, Why art thou wroth? and why is thy countenance fallen? If thou doest well, shalt thou not be accepted? and if thou doest not well, sin lieth at the door.

"And Cain talked with Abel his brother: and it came to pass, when they were in the field, that Cain rose up against Abel his brother, and slew him. And the Lord said unto Cain, Where is Abel, thy brother? And he said, I know not: Am I my brother's keeper?"[1]

When the Lord asked the people of Afra if they would be willing to lay down their lives for their kinsmen and friends, their answer was the same as Cain's: "Am I my brother's keeper?"

The one who answers "no" to that question is dedicated to his ego. He will never be his brother's keeper, and eventually the divine spark within him will die—the threefold flame will go out.

The threefold flame is the spiritual flame located in the heart chakra, the spiritual center within the chest cavity. In past golden ages, this flame was the size of a man and magnificent to behold. In most of mankind today, the threefold flame is a mere one-sixteenth of an inch in height, but the flame can be expanded through devotion and service to life. The power that resides in the threefold flame can change the world. The flame can also be further diminished, and even snuffed out, through continual anger and resentment.

The Threefold Flame

Afra knew that many of his people had lost their threefold flame, just as many people today are losing their threefold flame through anger and discord. He knew that in order to regain that flame, they would have to follow a path of brotherhood. They would have to care for one another with a deep soul-caring, a profound love that comes from the Holy Spirit as a ray of light directly from the heart of God.

The only way he could teach them to be a brother to all others, was to be a brother to all himself.

This he did. And for this example, he was crucified by his own people. This is often the way of the world—brother does not recognize brother, and instead, the people determine to destroy the example of the path of personal Christhood that is before their very eyes. Jesus also set the example of Christhood before us, and for this, the people sought to destroy him.

Afra was the Christ in the midst of his own people, but they knew him not. They were blinded by their greed for power. They sought human power as well as the power of fallen angels.

Thus, rejected by his people, Afra departed that scene. He returned to the heart of God in the ritual of the ascension, becoming the ascended master whom we know today simply as Afra, our brother of light. ❧

Afra's Role Today

As an ascended master, Afra continues to work with the angels, brothers of light and the Higher Self of his brothers and sisters around the world for the unity of all mankind. Afra considers all people of the world, regardless of their race or nationality or religion, to be a part of the brotherhood of man. He is particularly concerned with black people everywhere and with the destiny of black people in Africa and America.

Afra stresses the theme of unity and of dissolving our differences in the fire of the Holy Spirit. He says: "We are brethren because we are of the same Mother.

"I am your brother, not your lord, not your master. I am your brother on the Path. I have shared your passion for freedom. I have shared with you the hours of crisis when you beheld injustice, when you prayed to the Lord for justice and the Lord gave to you the divine plan for this nation and for this continent.

"I have lived in your hearts for hundreds of years as you have toiled under the burden of oppression self-imposed from within and put upon from without.

"The people of Afra have the supreme opportunity to learn from every civilization and every history. When materialization reaches its peak, there are only two courses open to a civilization: either material decline and decay because of indulgence, or spiritual transcendence through the alchemy of the Holy Spirit."[2]

Dissolving Our Differences in the Holy Spirit

In order to have the Holy Spirit and to dissolve our differences in the Holy Spirit, as Afra teaches, we must give up our desire for human power and human prominence. We each contain within us the seed of Christ, known as the Holy Christ Self. We must let the Christ in us go before us as we step back and watch the miracles that the Holy Christ Self, the Lord and Saviour Jesus Christ, will perform in our name.

If we want revenge more than we want the Holy Spirit, we will be lost in the miasma and the mists that still hang over the continent of Africa. We may have to reincarnate again and again and again to learn these lessons. The choice is ours. We can choose to be Cain or we can choose to be Abel—the point of Antichrist or Christ.

Heaven is impartial: there are marvelous and holy people in every nation, in every race, in every religion. We cannot categorize people— there is no group entirely good or entirely evil, as the relative conditions of human consciousness go.

Nor are the masters concerned with the color of another's skin. Regarding the color of the coats of flesh that men wear, Afra says: "It does not matter. I do not know. And I am not concerned. And you ought not to be concerned either."[3]

When we have the Holy Spirit, we will not have a sense of what body we are in. Instead, we will have the clothing and that mantle that comes to us through the flame of our immortality itself. That flame is the threefold flame of everlasting life.

A Message for Afra's Descendants in America

One of Afra's brothers in heaven is the master Saint Germain. (His name, *Sanctus Germanus,* means simply, "holy brother".) Saint Germain carries the flame of freedom for all peoples on earth. Afra conveys the following message from Saint Germain to the descendants of Afra in America:

Saint Germain

"In this moment, those who call themselves the blacks of America can rise to new dimensions of freedom and liberty. But this can only come to pass through the mighty heart flame, through the understanding of the path of initiation under the Holy Spirit, through submitting yourself, your soul, to the altar of God and calling upon the Lord for an acceleration of light, a purging of inner darkness.

"Though there were successes through the civil rights movement, there have been setbacks. For those successes in many instances were outer. Having gained them, the people did not understand that they must go within to the inner light in order to sustain them. We would seek the equality of all souls whatever their outer 'color.' We would teach you a spiritual path of true advancement on the path of initiation.

"Though they know it not, the black people of America today are at the eternal Y. They must choose this day whom they will serve—whether gains in the line of material comfort and increased well-being and higher-paying jobs, or the real gain of the eternal light of Sonship and the path of immortality with all of its challenges. In this land of abundance, it is natural for all people to expect and to live according to a higher standard of living. It is when this higher standard obliterates the inner longing for the higher light and the higher way, that it becomes dangerous. I would tell you that God has chosen this people as those who have become rich in Spirit."[4]

In this long history and the cultural heritage of golden ages is the key to the destiny of the sons and daughters of Afra—including our black brothers and sisters in America. Afra teaches the way of real freedom through self-mastery.

In America today, freedom must be won by the choice to be. Saint Germain has said, "He who chooses not to be, becomes the slave of him who chooses to be."[5]

The choice to be or not to be is a choice that is played out in everyday life, within all of the races. Those who have a strong identity are those who rule. The challenge of life is to choose to be in God the master of oneself. When you are the master of yourself, you cannot be the slave of any.

The Cause of Racial Strife

The ascended master El Morya says, "I do not believe that division is the divine intent. I do not believe that manipulators do not exist in the world. I know that they exist, and that they exist to the total degradation of man."[6]

Jesus delivered the same message when he explained the mystery of the tares among the wheat. He said, "The good seed are the children of the kingdom; but the tares are the children of the wicked one; the enemy that sowed them is the devil."[7]

We find throughout history that racial strife has its origin in the divide-and-conquer tactics of these who are called the fallen ones. These are they who, by choice, by free will, have taken what is known as the left-handed path. They appear in every race and in every nation. The ascended masters call them "the spoilers" because wherever there is light, true religion and joy, they come to spoil that pure and holy innocent vibration of the good seed. These fallen ones have used race to divide the children of God on earth, and it is time that this lie be exposed!

It was through these divide-and-conquer tactics that the great light, the golden age, on the continent of Africa was initiated. This episode in cosmic history is described in *Climb the Highest Mountain*:

"To accomplish the breakdown of order, it is necessary to invert every other quality of God in man and in society: love must be turned into hatred; peace into war; truth into error; faith into doubt, fear and suspicion; and the sweet wine of Holy Communion into the bitter fruit of psychic intercourse.

"These perversions are systematically enforced through infiltrating God-government, education, science, and religion, the family, the church and the community with the warped concepts of warped minds. The authors of these perversions of the God flame have one goal in mind: the destruction of man and society through the dethroning of the Real Image"[8]— the image of Christ within.

What happened on the continent of Africa unfolds:

"By employing distraction and confusion as alternate weapons, the very few have turned the many upon this planetary home away from the main issues of life and the central order of the universe. The masterminds who brought down the children of Africa and an ancient civilization of great light that once flourished on what has come to be known as 'the dark continent,' did so through the perversion of its sacred rituals and art forms. By injecting distortions of the divine art into the consciousness of the people, they were able to capture their minds and emotions and to divert their attention from the Presence,* causing their energies to flow into matrices of dense desire.

"As time went on, the people lost the wisdom of their ancestors, worshiping those they should have emulated. The accounts of sacred

---

*The individualized Presence of God.

powers wielded by their forebears became folk-lore. All forgot that long ago they, too, had been entrusted with the secrets of the universe. Thus, the history of a people who perished for want of vision is written in akasha[9]—a dramatic portray-al of the cultural sinking of a continent.

"What happens to a people who lose the light that once rendered transparent the very cells of their bodies, is most pitiful to behold. Ultimately, the ubiquitous rhythm of the jungle reduced their beings to a primitive state, and the tie that had held these children of Mu in orbit around the golden sun of Cosmic Christ illumination was broken. Truly darkness covered the face of the land."[10]

Today, we are witnessing the return of the light and the Mother flame to the continent of Afra. The children of Afra are responding to the fires of freedom. The masters pray that they choose to be the Christed ones and manifest the victory for all.

Humility

Afra teaches that humility is a key ingredi-ent of the path of brotherhood. Like all true masters, Afra is an example of true humility.

Another humble brother, the ascended master Kuthumi, once embodied as Saint Francis, speaks of Afra's humility:

"This giant soul with his tremendous devotion was one of the unknown brothers. So long as individuals feel the need to expound upon their own personal achievements, they may well find that they are not truly a part of us."[11]

The truly humble person is contemptible to anyone who retains the ego, who retains personal pride, because there is nothing that so exposes that ego, that not-self, than the presence of utter humility.

Pride takes many forms and true humility but one. True humility must be worn eternally. It is not a garment you place upon yourself for a moment, for a day or a year or when passing a test. It is an undergarment with which God himself is clothed, and unless it surrounds the disciple, the hopes of attainment are slim indeed.

Humility is a face that shines and glows with such light as to have no need to glory in itself. It has literally been taken up into that radiant life and knows no other life but God and claims no other self but God.

Brotherhood

God is in all men's hearts, and all men are brothers, made of one blood.* The true understanding of "Who is my brother?" has been explained in countless parables and inspired writings. Jesus explained that "Whosoever doeth the will of God, the same is my brother, and my sister, and mother"[12]—and in reality, the brother, the sister, and mother of all life. Thus, all men are brothers under the Father-Mother God.

The tenets of most faiths support the statement "I AM my brother's keeper"; and this is as it should be, for, in reality all life is one. The scientific corollary to this truth is found in the statement of Jesus "Inasmuch as ye have done it unto one of the least of these my brethren, ye have done it unto me"[13]—unto the Christ-identity of all men.

True brotherhood is found in the flame of the Mother. All men are brothers because they are born of the same spiritual mother; and all ascend-

---

*"[God] hath made of one blood all nations of men for to dwell on the face of the earth." (Acts 17:26.)

ed masters are devotees of that Mother flame.

The light of the Mother is the light in the aura of all of God's people. It is manifest in the chakras, or spiritual centers, as the light of the Kundalini, rising from the base of the spine to the crown. The Mother flame is the energy of all creation

In the unity of brotherhood, all people, no matter what their race or origin, can give these affirmations with the master Afra:

Affirmations for Brotherhood

I walk in the footsteps of Afra.

I AM a brother, a sister to all.

I comfort. I console.

I AM true to myself and to my God.

I bear the honor of God in my heart.

I enter into mystical union with the Holy Spirit.

I AM one with the Prince of Peace.

I shall walk in the Spirit from this day on.

For this is the day of my victory.

This is my hour and the power of light.

I shall lead my people to the throne of glory.

Receive me now, O God!

The Law of Cause and Effect—Karma among the Nations

The fundamental law that people of every nation wrestle with daily is the law of cause and effect, the law of karma. All have free will, yet all are accountable for their actions. If by free will we hurt another part of life, then the Law itself, impersonal, returns to us that momentum of hurt—not to punish, but to give us the experience that teaches us that we limit ourselves each time we limit another.

For example, if we send forth anger, that anger is like a boomerang, and it returns to us—sometimes quickly, sometimes more slowly. The energy goes forth from the chakras in anger, and the anger must return to us because we sent it forth. This returning energy can manifest in many ways—a headache, depression, some kind of ill fortune, maybe even in the form of a sudden accident. The energy of anger is very powerful. It is destructive to the one to whom it is sent, and it is even more destructive to the one who sends it forth.

Jesus bore the sins of mankind, which means that he bore mankind's returning karma—for sin and karma are synonymous terms. Afra also went through the crucifixion for the love of his people. He bore the cross as Jesus did, and the bearing of the cross simply means the bearing of the weight of world karma.

This was the burden he bore for love of his people. In this day and age, Afra asks us to bear one another's burden, just as Jesus admonished us.

What is our burden? Our burden is always our karma. That is why we often feel heavy. Even the heaviness of the gravitation of the earth is actually an effect of planetary karma. The full weight of all transgressions upon the Law of God of all humanity of all centuries remains— until it is transmuted, until it is consumed by the sacred fire in answer to our call.

Karma is the reason it is so difficult to

resolve planetary problems. This is why people never seem able to stop their disputes in the Middle East. They cannot get over their arguments, because they are based on an ancient karma. They need to give up the desire to conquer the other one, to get even for something that was done to them in the past.

When will they ever get through? When will they ever cease getting even for something that happened a half a century and more ago? One has to forgive in order to be free of one's past karma. One has to say, "We will not go on killing to get even for what happened a century ago or ten thousand years ago." You will never be free from karma if you have never forgiven someone who did something to you or your ancestors.

According to God's laws, those who have certain burdens of karma through misuse of the Law must have those above them who are of greater attainment and light to intercede, since each one of us is limited by the weight of our karma as to what the outpouring of light may be from God.

Now this may seem unfair or unjust, but it is not. Those who have proven themselves responsible with the use of God's light and energy, have access to more light. This is the meaning of the words of Jesus: "Unto every one which hath shall be given; and from him that hath not, even that he hath shall be taken away from him."[14] Thus, those who have light and who have used that light responsibly, shall be given more light, and they will be able to assist those who have lost their own light through misusing it. Afra is one master who can intercede in the karma of the nations.

The sons and daughters of Afra in Africa, in America and in all nations can take the teachings of the ascended masters and the spiritual tools they have released and use them for the liberation of the tremendous love and light God has given them. ⚜

SECTION II
Spiritual Tools for Unity and Brotherhood

Prayer and the Science of the Spoken Word

Afra has said, "You must give forth in your spoken Word the commands of God for unity." The call compels the answer, and for thousands of years the mystics of East and West have connected with the power of creation through prayer and by repeating spoken mantras and the names of God. You can also use prayer and affirmations to create spiritual and material changes in your life and the world around you.

The science of the spoken Word is a gift of the Divine Mother that you can use to heal yourself and the planet. It is a system of powerful affirmations, or worded formulas, called decrees. Prayer is like a conversation with God, where we send to him our dreams, our hopes, our wishes, and ask him to enter our lives. The decree is the means whereby the kingdom of God becomes a reality here and now through the power of the spoken Word.

No matter what your belief system, you can add decrees to your devotions. The science of the spoken Word, or decreeing, is the most effective and powerful way to harness God's energy. It is the key to changing yourself and the world.

You can use the following decree by Kuthumi to send God's light and love into the world. As you say the words, visualize yourself as a being of light and see this light going into the trouble spots of the world to bring unity and brotherhood.

When you say the words "I AM" in this decree, you are using the name that God revealed to Moses. You are really saying "God in me is."*

---

* "And God said unto Moses…Thus shalt thou say unto the children of Israel, I AM hath sent me unto you." (Exod. 3:14.)

I AM Light by Kuthumi

I AM light, glowing light,
Radiating light, intensified light.
God consumes my darkness,
Transmuting it into light.

This day I AM a focus of the Central Sun.
Flowing through me is a crystal river,
A living fountain of light
That can never be qualified
By human thought and feeling.
I AM an outpost of the Divine.
Such darkness as has used me is
    swallowed up
By the mighty river of light which I AM.

I AM, I AM, I AM light;
I live, I live, I live in light.
I AM light's fullest dimension;
I AM light's purest intention.
I AM light, light, light
Flooding the world everywhere I move,
Blessing, strengthening and conveying
The purpose of the kingdom of heaven.

The Violet Flame for the Violet Race

One of the spiritual keys that Afra recommends is the use of the violet flame. The violet flame has been seen by seers, mystics and saints. It is the seventh-ray aspect of the Holy Spirit—a spiritual flame that carries a high, spiritual energy. It is also the flame that is revealed in the Aquarian age.

Saint Germain teaches the accelerated path of transmutation of karma by the violet flame of the Holy Spirit. Through the violet flame and service to life we can transcend the rounds of rebirth. The use of the violet flame can help us greatly on the path of individual Christhood leading to the ascension.

In the East, there is also the awareness of the Trinity of God, which they know as Brahma, Vishnu and Shiva—the Creator, the Preserver and the Destroyer.

The Holy Spirit corresponds to Shiva, the third person of the Hindu Trinity. Shiva is the Destroyer, the one who breaks down the misqualified energies, or the misuses of life that we have brought forth by our misuse of free will. For example, we have free will to qualify God's energy as love or as hatred. If we have qualified it as hatred, that energy rests with us. It remains with us as part of our consciousness until we transmute it by love. The power of the Holy Spirit to transmute hatred into love manifests by this dispensation of the violet flame.

We can invoke the violet flame by giving a simple mantra where we affirm the name of God, I AM, and then declare that that I AM is the violet flame right where we are. This mantra can increase the manifestation of the violet flame within our aura:

I AM a being of violet fire!
I AM the purity God desires!

This little mantra becomes a meditation and a visualization that is anchored in the physical body by the spoken Word. Giving word to our thoughts and our feelings through the throat chakra is the means whereby we gain a new dimension from our prayers and our mental affirmations. Through the throat chakra we bring into physical form that which is in the mind and that which is in the heart.

When people begin to give these mantras, they experience an immediate acceleration of consciousness. The violet flame, then, is the first step on the path of initiation with the ascended masters, the first step toward the point of the return of the soul to the Spirit, or to the I AM Presence.

Afra recommends the use of the violet flame to dissolve discord, envy and jealousy within the family, schoolyard and community and in the governments of the world. ✤

The Healing Power
of Forgiveness

Afra has asked us to forgive and be forgiven. Forgiveness is an aspect of the violet flame and an essential part of the healing of the nations. He has said forgiveness is an important step on the spiritual path. If we skip forgiveness, we will need to retrace our steps. If we are holding on to those things that are a burden to our souls, we need to let them go through the healing power of forgiveness.

People sometimes worry that if they forgive someone, then that person won't get the just punishment they ought to receive. The one who has been wronged may not want to let the situation go, because they are absolutely certain that the wrongdoer must have their just deserts.

But the law of karma is unfailing, and God and his Law will take care of all our wrongdoing. God says, "Vengeance is mine; I will repay."[1] God is just, and he deals justly with everyone. Let God worry about that person and their sins. God does his job, and we have to do our job. Our job is to forgive, because forgiveness frees us.

Hatred is binding. Non-forgiveness is enslaving. In the end, if we do not forgive, we become the prisoners of our non-forgiveness. The North American Indians had an important ritual. They gathered around the fire at night, talked things over, put everything that had occurred that day into the flame, both physical and spiritual, accepted that it was over—and then it was finished. It was a way of calling upon the law of forgiveness. This ritual enabled them to start the new day with a clean, white page.

The world's great spiritual traditions all teach forgiveness as the key to inner peace, and the law of forgiveness is a universal law. Jesus used this law when he forgave before he healed. He often said "Thy sins be forgiven thee. Go and sin no more."[2] He also demonstrated the supreme example of forgiveness on the cross, when he said, "Father, forgive them; for they know not what they do."[3]

Psychotherapist and author Robin Casarjian in her book *Forgiveness: A Bold Choice for a Peaceful Heart* says:

"Forgiveness is a required course for all of us. There is no way for us to have world peace without it. Forgiveness gives each of us the immediate power to play a vital and necessary part in a planetary peacemaking and evolutionary process. If enough individuals choose to live from their heart for more and more moments, perhaps we will reach that critical mass when world healing is not only possible, but inevitable."[4]

Forgiveness is the element of grace that was not present until the coming of Jesus. With Moses there was only the Law. That law was the law of karma—the instantaneous descent of karma to the children of Israel when they disobeyed God. With the coming of Jesus, we entered a different era. We have greater access to the Higher Self, the personal Christ Self, and greater access to grace and mercy and forgiveness. Therefore, the Lord's Prayer says, "And forgive us our debts, as we forgive our debtors."[5]

Anger, hatred and resentment are binding. Anyone who hates is bound to the object of their hatred as surely as if they had tied themselves to that person with a rope. They cannot stop talking about or thinking about that person and how they are going to get even.

Mankind cannot stand in the presence of their Higher Self if they have withheld forgiveness from any part of life. Hatred and nonforgiveness bind us to that which we hate and separate us from our own Higher Self. As we resolve with one another, God resolves with us. We enter into the state of oneness whereby we can have greater personal freedom, we can precipitate the abundance we desire to have in our lives and we can do more than we were able to do before.

Forgiveness and the Law of Karma

When we forgive, we feel lighter because we are freer—the tangled mess of ropes has been removed, and we are free to love and move and embrace life again in a way that we could not do before. When we hate any part of life, whether ourself or another person or group of people, we are really hating God.* God is literally imprisoned inside the one whom we hate until we set that one free.

As we forgive others, so we may also receive forgiveness—both from our fellowman and from God. But if all is forgiven, what happens to the sin itself?

From a spiritual perspective, we find that forgiveness merely sets aside a debt and gives us time to pay it off. But it does not dissolve our responsibility for misdeeds, for breaking the laws of God or misuses of the sacred fire. It provides renewed opportunity for us to make things right.

We should not take the opportunity of forgiveness for granted. There comes a time when, if we constantly call for forgiveness but we fail to forsake sin, then this command is no longer obeyed by the cosmic forces of life. It is therefore important to get in a right relationship with

---

* "Inasmuch as ye have done it unto one of the least of these my brethren, ye have done it unto me." (Matt. 25:40)

our Higher Self, so that we can change our lives and no longer make the same mistakes.

All of these lessons, when understood, lead back to the knowledge of the science of the spoken Word. It is the means whereby we can invoke the violet flame and the mercy of God to transmute karma, to dissolve records of sin and to liberate us from our past mistakes. As God has said, "I will remember their sin no more."[6]

God does not desire that anyone be eternally shackled to a mistake made a thousand years ago or yesterday. When we have seen the lesson, experienced the sorrow of our ignorance or our impetuousness, and sincerely desire to go on to a new level, God forgives. Then we have the opportunity, not only to go and sin no more, but to do those positive acts that are constructive toward life.

Forgiving Oneself

Often the hardest person to forgive is ourself. We are not really free when we are burdened with the sense that we are a bad person or that we made a mistake ten years ago, and it can never be washed from our garments because it's an eternal blot. If that concept is carried a few steps further—if we have ten, twenty, or fifty blots on our garment, soon we assume—or the devil will come along and tell us—that we will be condemned to eternal damnation.

Then the person may say, "Well, as long as I am already damned and condemned and can never rise again, I might as well go out and do anything. I might as well do it all—murder, rape, sell drugs, destroy other parts of life. Others have it good. They're going to heaven; I am not. So why don't I just let them have a little of the evil part of me while I am around?"

The soul is very unhappy in the state of feeling that it cannot rise again. Yes, Jesus died for our sins, but Jesus also said, "My Father worketh hitherto, and I work."[7]

We have to do our part. We can work with God, and in fact, it is the God in us that does the work. With God, we can build something new and better.

Forgiveness and the Spiritual Path

It is hard to make spiritual progress without forgiveness. Forgiveness is freeing—it frees us, and it frees the other person. But forgiveness and freedom can only come when there is a change of heart, a change of spirit and soul.

It takes a lot to say, "I am no longer going to hold this thing against you. You burned my house down. You caused the death of my mother. You did all these things to me." Either you let go of it and put it into the flame, or you can carry it with you for ten lifetimes. You may not remember why you hate this person, but when you meet him, you hate him on sight, because in your soul you have never forgiven, you have never resolved, you have never put it into the flame, and you are bound by that hatred. And you are binding the other person or a whole nation.

If we never forgive people for what they have done to us, we will remain bound. If the nations do not forgive one another, they will remain bound. It's as simple as that. At some point we have to say, "Christ is greater than all these things," and realize that being wronged is really a test to see if we can contain the quality of mercy, if we can be Christlike, or are we a follower of Christ in lip-service only? If we can't forgive, how can we call ourselves followers of Christ?

The measure of our discipleship and spirituality is how much we love. The psychology of the carnal mind, or the lesser self, says to us, "You cannot be forgiven, and God is not willing to forgive you." But God has said he will wipe the slate clean. And he can, and he will, if we ask for forgiveness.

If we have wronged another person, we may need to go to them and ask for forgiveness and seek to right the wrong, if possible. Serve the person in some way or serve others who are suffering or who are less fortunate. Make amends, pray and ask for forgiveness.

If we cannot forgive, we can pray fervently for a change of heart. If necessary, get counseling from a qualified counselor or a minister. And we can use the violet flame for forgiveness. Many have found that it really works.

Here is a simple mantra for forgiveness:

> I AM forgiveness acting here,
> Casting out all doubt and fear,
> Setting men forever free
> With wings of cosmic victory.
>
> I AM calling in full power
> For forgiveness every hour;
> To all life in every place
> I flood forth forgiving grace.

When you forgive, you forgive the soul, but you are not condoning an action of wrongdoing. Forgiveness never means condoning behaviors that are unacceptable or abusive. Ours is to forgive and not to judge. We can love the soul, and we can forgive the person for what they have done, but we do not love and forgive the act that is counter to the laws of God and man.

Nor does forgiveness mean that we do not seek restitution or expect the other person to take accountability and responsibility for their actions. If we ask for accountability in a spirit of love and forgiveness, we can help the other person to balance their karma and come to a higher understanding.

Forgiveness does not mean that we abandon common sense or that we now do not take a course of action that can change the course of events for the better. As Robin Casarjian says:

"Because we forgive a nation, it doesn't mean that we, as a nation, eliminate all existing weapons and dismantle the military as a show of good faith—for, in reality, there are obviously peoples and leaders of nations who, disowning their own anger and inner conflicts, have a need to project it outward, often in the form of military might. With groups as with individuals, forgiving is not about what we do; it is about where we come from in thought and action. By forgiving, we participate in ways that contribute to positive and peaceful outcomes."[8] ❧

Afra Can Intercede in World Conditions

Afra says: "Call to me. I am just a knock away." We can pray to him to bring his momentum for unity into the world. We can ask him to dissolve racial tensions through the true understanding of universal brotherhood. His presence is sorely needed in a world where we see brother turning against brother and nation against nation.

Afra can bring divine solutions to seemingly unsolvable problems—whether in the age-old tensions in the Middle East or the India-Pakistan conflict or in racial divisions in the major cities of the world or community struggles anywhere on earth.

The master Afra is a strategist. Invite him to be present spiritually wherever important decisions are being made for world peace, or wherever meetings are taking place on a national or international level. The master can overshadow those who meet to decide the fate of nations.

He is pledged to help solve the problems of divergent peoples, local wars, strife in religion, strife between the Arabs and the Jews, between the blacks and the whites and the Christians and the Moslems.

Afra says: "I will be with you! I will speak through you, and together we will turn back these fallen ones who have determined to destroy the cities of America and America as a whole by this division and by discontent and riot and all that shall not be, because we are determined that it shall not be and that they shall not pass!" ✤

Prayer for Brotherhood

Out of the One,
Thou, God, hast spun
All of the races of men.
By thy great Law
Do thou now draw
All to their God Source again.

Take away hate;
By love abate
All mankind's vicious intent.
Show thy great pow'r
Every hour
Of love and compassion God sent.

I AM, I AM, I AM
Divine love sending forth
The wonderful feeling of true divine
    healing,
Unguents of light now sealing
All of the schisms of men.

Stop all division!
By God-precision
Love is the hallowed law-key.
Ultimate peace,
Make all war cease,
Let the children of men now go free!

Stop mankind's friction,
All their predictions
Tearing bless'd heart from heart.
By God-direction
Produce now perfection
In thy great family—one heart.

SECTION III
Words from the Master

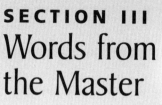

Afra Speaks

This section of the book contains the discourses given by the ascended master Afra through the messenger Elizabeth Clare Prophet.

God has always had messengers and prophets. For almost 40 years, Elizabeth Clare Prophet has been a messenger of God. Throughout her career, she has received messages from many saints and angels, East and West, whom we know as the ascended masters.

The Role of the Messenger

In The *Astrology of the Four Horsemen*, Elizabeth Clare Prophet describes her role as messenger:

"My calling is to be a prophet of God. *Prophet* means one who speaks for God, hence a messenger. Coincidentally (although I don't believe in coincidences), my name matches my calling. Prophet is the surname of my late husband and teacher, Mark L. Prophet. It was the family name that had been carried through generations from France to Ireland to Canada to Chippewa Falls, Wisconsin.

"Mark was a prophet and a messenger, called by God through the ascended master El Morya to found The Summit Lighthouse in Washington, D.C., in 1958. He was and is the most amazing person I've ever met—the most humble, the most holy, the most human.

"We were together for 12 years, were married, had four children, wrote many books, lectured around the world and built our movement. And then he passed on in 1973, his soul now one with God, yet ever with me.

"In 1964 I received the 'mantle' of messenger, including gifts of the Holy Spirit. And throughout my ministry, by God's grace, I have built upon the foundation of prophetic teachings already laid by my husband.

"As a messenger of God, I see myself as the servant of God's light within you. And the servant is not greater than his lord.[1] My Lord is the Christ of Jesus and the Christ of you, who are one and the same. For as John the Beloved wrote, that Christ was and is 'the true Light, which lighteth every man that cometh into the world.'[2] Therefore, I come as a servant of that light—your light, my light, your Christ, my Christ."[3]

Mrs. Prophet describes the process whereby she receives messages from God, the masters and angels:

"I receive this prophecy through the power of the Holy Spirit in the manner of the ancient prophets and apostles. When the transmission is about to take place, I enter a meditative state and attune with the Lord God or his representative. The Lord's presence or that of an ascended master, a cosmic being or an archangel comes upon me, and the words and the light flow in a power and a personality not my own.

"This congruency of my soul with the living Word of God I call a dictation, for the words are being dictated to me even as I am speaking them in the vibration of the divine speaker. It is truly a divine happening of which I am but the instrument. It is a gift of the Holy Spirit and not something I can make happen…. The only way to describe this experience is to say, in the words of the prophet: 'The Spirit of the Lord God is upon me.' "[4]

The dictations you are about to read contain the light and energy of the master. The words are his teaching, but they are also cups for the consciousness of the master. The spiral of light within the words is for your quickening and spiritual initiation. As you read the words, ask for the Presence of the master Afra to be with you and guide your understanding and help you to apply his teaching in your life. His teaching is vital to the times in which we live. ⚜

The Powers and Perils
of Nationhood

The first dictation by the ascended master Afra was delivered in Accra, Ghana, in 1976. The nations of Africa were at a turning point. Having recently secured independence from colonial rule, they had many choices before them: What model of economic development would they pursue? What system of government? Would they allow old conflicts between different tribes to resurface? Or would they rise to a new freedom and unity?

The Powers and Perils of Nationhood

Salutations in the flame of Afra! Let light *flow* unto a continent and unto a people! Let light flow from the fiery core of the I AM THAT I AM, from the side of the north unto the side of the south. Let the light descend from the crown unto the base. And let the fulfillment of the Father-Mother God be the reuniting of all peoples upon this continent. By the sacred fire of the Holy Spirit, let them be united in love under the banner of Micah, the angel of Unity, who also united the children of Israel and also united the people of America in time of civil war with the banner *Union* and with the cry, "Remember ye are brethren."[5]

I call to the children of Afra. "All your strength is in your union. All your danger is in discord."[6] So were the words of Hiawatha unto the tribes of the Indians. And by the smoking of the peace pipe and the smoking of the lamps of God, the union of the sacred fire brought together the divergent tribes, and they became as one—one in the consciousness of God, one out of many, *e pluribus unum*.[7] So, one people out of many nations and origins and tribes.

Let Differences Be Dissolved in the Flame of Love

So as the individual yields to the family, as the family yields to the community, and as the community yields to the nation, let it be that in this hour of the coming of the Lord's Spirit in the descent of the fire of the Holy Ghost, the differences of the peoples of this continent shall be dissolved in the one flame of love. Let the gift of the Holy Spirit be the understanding of tongues—not only of the speech but of the heart and the mind and the soul.

Let the people understand we are brethren

because we are of the same Mother. Let Mother and the love of Mother be the flow. How can you kill when you kill the one who has come forth from the same womb of Mother? Out of the womb of the Cosmic Virgin, out of time and space you came forth as mighty conquerors, as teams of conquerors of old, as the blue race and the violet race. So you came and so you are one in the light of Alpha and Omega, the beginning and the ending, the first and the last, the one unity.[8] So, out of one, many; so, many is the coming of the one.

The Only True Slavery Is the Slavery from Within

I am your brother—not your lord, not your master, but I am your brother on the Path. I have shared your passion for freedom. I have shared with you the hours of crisis when you beheld injustice, when you sought the Lord and prayed to him for justice and the Lord gave to you the divine plan for this nation and for this continent.

I have lived in your hearts these hundreds and hundreds of years as you have toiled under the burden of oppression from within and without. And although many have considered the outer oppression the greater, we who are among those who have graduated from this continent consider that the only true slavery is the slavery from within—the slavery of the carnal mind and its selfishness, its failure to sacrifice upon the altar as Abraham and Isaac sacrificed. So, the failure to sacrifice the beasts of the carnal mind: this is slavery.

Now then, it is because some have been willing to make the sacrifice of selfishness that the outer slavery has also been broken, and it is the evolution of the people themselves toward the light of God that has given this new opportunity in this age to this continent.

I Come Because You Have Called to Me

I come because you have called to me, because you are the ones who are awake with the Lord Buddha, the ones who are aware of the God flame. Without the call there can be no answer, but the call does indeed compel the answer. You have compelled the presence of the messenger so that you could hear in the power of the spoken Word my communication, which you have felt in your hearts already and which you have known in your minds to be the presence of the angels and the archangels and the hosts of the Lord who have come to you to give you grace and protection and comfort in all ways and in all generations.

I come, then, that you might see the great flow of the merging of the peoples in the river of the water of life that is the flow of Mother. In the crystal flow of Mother light from the base chakra to the crown of a continent, there is the merging of the people.

And so as Mother Liberty came to the shores of America on behalf of her son Saint Germain to anoint the pilgrims who came to that land, to ignite in them the flame of the heart that they might be called the people of America—from every nation, from every origin, ethnic and racial, they came. They left behind their differences, they became one nation because Mother Liberty, standing in the harbor of New York, holding the torch high, kindled in their hearts that flame of oneness with the same message of the angel Micah: "Remember ye are brethren. I am your Mother; I have begotten thee." This is what makes an American: it is a common flame, a common devotion, a common freedom.

This is what shall come to pass as the people of Africa take the torch of freedom. It is the coming of Mother Liberty, it is the anointing of the hearts, it is the conveyance of the three-fold flame. It is the coming of the Ancient of Days with the threefold flame, espoused by the sons and daughters of Venus and of other planets in this system of worlds.[9] The threefold flame of the Trinity is the unifying factor of the nations.

Forge the Identity of a Continent

Let them leave their nets, let them leave their weapons, let them come at the calling of the Lord and let them hear the call. Let them see the vision, let them have the mind of Afra, let their minds be united in the mandala of a continent. And out of that fiery core of God and of the God design, let them forge first the identity in Christ, then the identity in family, then the identity in community, then the identity in nation, then the identity of a continent.

When you examine the facts of existence in these nations in this hour, it is a bit different from the vision that I bring. Divergent peoples, local wars, strife in religion, strife between the Arabs and the Jews, between the blacks and the whites and the Christians and the Moslems.

O beloved hearts! There is a groaning in the very soul and the heart of the World Mother for her children. There is the travail of the Divine Mother to give birth to the Christ consciousness when her children are moving against the very flow of life. Did not Jesus give forth the cry of his lamentation in that hour, "O Jerusalem, Jerusalem, thou that killest and stonest the prophets, how often I would have gathered thee under my wing as a hen gathereth her chicks, but ye would not!"[10]

So I say to you who are the people of God and who now have the torch passed to you of the science of the spoken Word, you must give forth in your spoken Word the commands of God for unity, for the alchemical fires of freedom to dissolve the differences of tribalism and the envy and the jealousy even in the family and in the schoolyard and in the community and in the government. Let all become servants of the one God and the one destiny.

The Powers of Nationhood

And these are the powers of nationhood: it is the power that is given to those who attain in the Christ, the power that was given to Jesus when he said, "All power is given unto me in heaven and in earth."[11] This power is accorded to every son and daughter of God who is the overcomer in the way—to every son and daughter of God who is the overcomer in the way. This is the power to forge the victory.

But there is a testing, a mighty testing, before the power is conveyed. It is the testing of Jesus in the wilderness; it is the offer of the fallen ones, the rebellious ones. The souls of the tares—the tares, the seed of the Wicked One sown among the good wheat—these are also among you and they come with their temptations. They show you the kingdoms of this world and they say, "All these things will we give you if you will fall down and worship us."[12]

You must stand steadfast in the hour, in the hour of the testing. You must be willing to fast with Jesus for Ghana, for Afra—fast from the desires and the things of this world so that you are not caught in the hour of the temptation to sell your soul for materialism.

For when the temptation has passed and you have resisted the temptation to command these stones be made bread, when you have resisted the temptation to cast yourself down the mountain to test the Lord, when you have resisted all things by the power of the Trinity, then and only then will the power of God be vouchsafed to you to build a new nation and a new continent conceived in the very heart of the Goddess of Liberty.

Afra's Prayer to the Father-Mother God

O Mother Liberty, teach thy children! I am Afra, a Son of God and a brother of this people. I kneel before you, O Divine Mother, O Woman clothed with the Sun, O counterpart of the Divine Father in heaven. I pray to thee, to the Father-Mother God, and I ask for the teachings of God to be given to this people so that they are not tempted with the powers of nationhood offered by the princes of this world who come from East and West, offering their proposals and tantalizing these who are the children of God who must yet mature to be sons and daughters of God.

O Alpha and Omega, give to them the courage to stand in the hour of the testing and to know that when they have gone through that dark night in Gethsemane and the morning is come and they are able to say with Jesus, "Father, let this cup pass from me: nevertheless not my will, but thine, be done"[13]—when they are able to say, "Not my will, but thine, be done," then will the angels of the Lord come and minister unto them and they will find that they are not alone and that they have within themselves the inner resources and the natural resources to conquer every foe, to meet every need, to solve every crisis.

Be Not a House Divided

But these resources come in union and in unity—not in the fragmentation but in the removing of the lines of division, beginning within the human soul. Let yourself not be a house divided against itself. Let there not be a warring in your members. But call in the name of God for the judgment of the archangels to come into your temple and into your house. And let your confirmation of the judgment be the casting out of the Fallen One and of the seed of the Wicked One and of the carnal mind. Let your light in Christ challenge the dragon and the beast that cometh out of the earth and out of the sea. Let it challenge, then, the false prophet, the Antichrist and the Great Whore. For your soul, one in Christ and one with God, can confirm the judgment that is outlined for you in the Revelation of John.[14]

See to it, then, that this fire of love as the fire of judgment, is received upon your heart's altar this day, and that each day to come you invoke that judgment through the Lord Christ. And thereby making yourself that one, that indivisible Christ manifestation, you will be the electrode for the making of this community of the Holy Spirit one nation. And then all nations coming together, each sitting under his own vine and fig tree[15]—all shall know the Lord from the least unto the greatest, all shall read the laws of God which are written in their inward parts.[16] Then it will be seen that the mandala—the very blueprint of the nations that is according to the law of karma—will make of each nation of this continent a contributor of self-worth, self-reliance and self-respect.

Place upon the Altar the Firstfruits of the Talents of the People

As each nation makes that contribution for the whole, placing upon the altar of Afra the firstfruits of the talents of the people—the resources, the industry, the government, the culture, the music, the art, the science—so all of these fruits of the harvest of the Lord, given in the day of the harvest as the testimony upon the altar, will be that acceptable offering of the son of God, of Abel the righteous.[17] And the smoke of that offering will rise unto the heavens and the Lord God will release the blessing, for you have brought unto his house the fullness of the tithe that is called from your heart, for which you are called in this age. This is the fire of the union, this is the meaning of sacrifice, this is the meaning of the sacrament and of the atonement.

And all these things shall come to pass in the Church of the Lord Christ that is established in heaven as on earth—the Church Universal and Triumphant, whose door is the heart of the Mother, open to all of her children regardless of conviction or origin or past association.

Choose You This Day Whom You Will Serve

I release to you the words of the love of my heart, but I also release to you the energies to infire this continent. The powers of nationhood can be either the power of the prince of this world or the power of the Son of God. With Joshua, the son of Nun, I say to you this day: Choose you this day whom you will serve![18] Then beware. Beware, for the emissaries of the prince of this world will come. Yea, they have already come bearing gifts of this world. But look for the coming of the emissaries of the sons and daughters of God. Receive them and know that they truly are the instruments of your own Self-realization, Self-elevation—*Self* in the True Self, which is Christ, the chief cornerstone of every house.[19]

And so in these powers are to be seen the perils of nationhood, that when the children are new to their freedom and their liberty, they look to imitate those who are the older cultures who have gone the way of their blueprint—some who have made mistakes, some who have followed the powers of the prince of this world, for they have entered into the temptation, and some who have followed the teachings of the Son of God.

Let the children of Afra look within and find the inner key to the God consciousness in this age. Let them be imitators of Christ and not imitators of the carnal minds of the other nations. So as the Christ has come forth in every nation, that Christ may be imitated here. So is power in him and in him alone. The knowledge of the peril of nationhood that I bring to you this day is the peril of the failure of the people to be obedient to the laws of God and to make the necessary sacrifices so that the whole can be won—forged and won.

The Peril of Selfishness and Absence of Vision

The great danger, then, the great peril to Ghana and to every nation is the danger of chaos and confusion that is born of selfishness, where there is no path, no way or truth or life as taught by the avatars, no desire for initiation in God, no realization that life is for testing, life is for the exercise of free will, life is for the balancing of karma, the fulfillment of dharma, and the return of the soul unto the altar of the Ancient of Days in the ritual of the ascension.

The peril of nationhood is the peril of the absence of vision, for without vision the people perish.[20] And the people lose their vision proportionately as they increase in self-indulgence, in selfishness, in the cults of success, ambition and pride.

This is a disease that begins in the leaders, that is transferred to the people, that is then increased in them and returned to the leaders until [the people of] the nation are at odds with one another and there is nothing but the spying on one another and the attempts at the coup to remove the statesmen and those who are in the position of leadership.

There is envy, there is jealousy, there is graft, there is greed, there is bribery. These are the perils of nationhood—when a people who have been deprived of their resources and of their energies, who have been enslaved to others for so many centuries, become drunk now with the wealth of their nation, become drunk with power and the desire to rule over one another. Have they so early forgotten that once all were common subjects of other masters? Have they forgotten that they are brethren?

Learn from Every Civilization and History

O this people! If you could see me as I walk the streets of Accra and of Ghana and of these nations, you would see me as the prophets of Israel of old! And I rend my garments for the sins of the people, for their failure to see that if they fail in this age to forge this union, then Afra will go down like the other powers and civilizations of this world have gone down—ever since the sinking of Lemuria and Atlantis, the days of Rome and Greece and ancient China and all of those civilizations who have come to naught because they have worshiped the god of Baal.

Let it be seen, then, that the hour for the coming of the victory on this continent is nigh. If you fail to accept the torch of liberty, if you fail to take with you the science of the spoken Word, if you fail to sacrifice the lesser self, then you will go the way of all the rest.

The people of Afra have the supreme opportunity to learn from every civilization and every history. They must learn that the peak of civilization at the point when the conquest of Matter has been attained—that peak must be met with the point of the capstone of the pyramid when the All-Seeing Eye of God translates the soul into a spiritualization of culture.

When civilization as materialization reaches its peak, there are only two courses that are open: either material decline and decay because of indulgence, or spiritual transcendence when, by the alchemy of the Holy Spirit, all that has been attained in Matter becomes the foundation of the pyramid whereby this attainment is transferred in Spirit and the people experience the new birth in Spirit and in Christ.

In this very hour, this moment of the

peaking of material attainment has come for many nations in East and West. In this moment the idling of the energies of God in the nexus of the cross of white fire is for these peoples to choose this day the Word of the Lord and the message of the prophets in every age, to choose to spiritualize consciousness. My friends, the choice is: To be or not to be!

It is not the case that "ye shall not surely die," as the serpent spoke those words.[21] It is the case when, surely as you choose, so will you be quickened unto everlasting life or judged at the judgment of God unto the second death.[22]

As the individual must make the choice, so nations must make the choice. So in this hour of the newness, the nations of Afra may choose to move forward on the parallel lines of the conquest of Matter and Spirit. Choosing wisely and well, they will not follow in the way of the destroyed planet Maldek, whose evolutions destroyed themselves in their ambition and their competition, which became the intense hatred of their laggard evolutions. Aye, planets and systems of worlds have been lost because evolutions have failed to make the choice.

People of Afra: Will You Make Your Choice?

Therefore, I stand before you this day. Heed my word on these powers and perils of nationhood that are before you. And remember my word. People of Afra: You must choose this day whom you will serve! You must choose to be or not to be. I ask you in the name of God, will you make your choice? [Audience responds: "Yes!"]

I thank you and I bid you adieu.

Comments by Elizabeth Clare Prophet following the dictation by Afra:

May I ask you who have the conviction in Christ to make the choice this day to be in God the fulfillment of the divine plan, to answer the question of Afra with the fiery statement, "I will!" Will you do that, please, to confirm that Word, you who will. [Audience responds: "I will!"]

Thank you. So by the spoken Word, you have confirmed the will to be. We are grateful for the depth of the wisdom of the masters, for the love of Afra that has brought him to us this day, and such a magnificent being! ✤

Ghana Class 1976
September 18, 1976
University of Legon
Accra, Ghana

For the Sons and
Daughters of Afra—
An Hour of Very Great
Opportunity and the
Drawing of the Line

In 1980, Afra spoke to his people again, this time at Camelot, the headquarters of The Summit Lighthouse, in the city of Los Angeles. In the four years since his last address there had been great changes on the continent of Africa, including a military coup in Ghana in which many members of the former government had been assassinated. Political instability or civil war continued in a number of nations. All of this the result of choices made—and not made.

Afra also speaks to his people in America with an assessment of what had been achieved in twenty-five years of the civil rights movement.

For the Sons and Daughters of Afra—An Hour of Very Great Opportunity and the Drawing of the Line

In joy I bow before the Lord of the World, Gautama Buddha. And I am most grateful to the Karmic Board, the Goddess of Liberty and Saint Germain for according me this opportunity to come to Camelot to answer the call of my chelas and to take the platform to deliver to you my address concerning the minority in America—the minorities of peoples who have come from many lands and continents and races and karmic origins.

Therefore, in the name of Lady Portia, I bow before the light within you, and I unveil myself as your own brother, Afra.

I come most recently from the continent of

Afra. I come from many lands troubled and in turmoil through strife. As the Nephilim upon that continent have sought to subjugate the peoples of the light, so I also understand that the key manipulation of divide and conquer has become a most intense overlay of hatred in defiance of the very person of our beloved and most noble Knight Commander, Saint Germain.

Saint Germain Is the Liberator of All Peoples

Saint Germain is the liberator of all peoples and streams of consciousness. He has drawn all together in the United States of America for the great birth and awakening of the Real and Eternal Self who is Christ the Lord. Therefore, we see in this hour—most perilous for Africa—division that begins with a hatred that has polarized and been placed upon the people even without their awareness of its influence as condemnation or pride or fear or belittlement or witchcraft or the vying for power that has been, much to our sorrow, the way of life there for many centuries.

Beloved Portia has made known to you the dedication of the ascended lady masters on behalf of the many islands of peoples who have gathered here seeking the flame of an inner identity, which, once attained, they are called by God to lay upon the altar of the community of the Holy Spirit that this nation was and is designed by Almighty God to be.[23]

Thus as you see, regrettably, the success that the fallen ones have had in duping the people of that continent, you may also project ahead and see that it is their desire to transfer these same momentums of division and superstition and witchcraft and hatred in this soil. We therefore come with love, intense love, and enlightenment and a mighty sword of Truth.

Chelas have arisen who understand this great need. And ever moving forward are the translations of Saint Germain's teachings into Spanish and the concern of those of you who are serving the light for those peoples who must have a very special interpretation of the God flame.

Saint Germain's Message for the Descendants of Afra

There is somewhat the sense of urgency as I meet in the Royal Teton with Saint Germain and others who serve him in the great cause of freedom. He has asked me to tell you today that concerning the descendants of Afra—those who live in the United States—this is an hour of very great opportunity as well as the drawing of the line.

In this moment, those who call themselves the blacks of America can rise to new dimensions of freedom and liberty. But this can only come to pass through the mighty heart flame, through the understanding of the path of initiation, through the necessity of bowing before the God flame of the Eternal Guru, submitting the self on the altar of God and demanding an acceleration, a purging, fervently calling upon the law of forgiveness as was preached by John the Baptist for you all—repentance and remission of sins,[24] then the coming of the Lord Christ and his initiation of the Christ Self.

Portia and Saint Germain desire that this

teaching should go forth among the blacks—
that they cannot rest with outer gains of more
opportunity or of laws that secure greater equality or even of increased funding for various
projects to enhance education and general standards of living. These signs must not be seen as
the signs of the elevation or necessarily even the
progress of a people.

And therefore, in an age of materialism and
mechanization, let not the outer signs become
mistaken for the inner sign of the coming of the
Lord Christ unto this my children. For it has
ever been the plot of the fallen ones to make all
peoples think that by the very manifestation of
increased goods or a greater climate of ease that
somehow progress is being made.

I Am Sending Forth a Ray from My Heart to Those Who Are the True Shepherds

Though there were successes through the
civil rights movement, there have been setbacks;
for those successes in many instances were
outer. Having gained them, the people did not
understand that they must go within to the

inner light in order to sustain them. Thus, it is not equality for bodies with varying colored skins that we would seek but true advancement on the path of initiation for souls who indeed hold the key for the entire elevation of this race of the sons and daughters of Afra.

I AM radiating in this hour a light ray from my heart to those who have been called long ago to be the shepherds of this people. Some of these shepherds-to-be are among this company of Camelot and others are yet abroad in the land serving with a great fervor of love and an understanding of justice, while those who are truly not qualified to lead yet somehow arrive in positions of leadership do serve—not with love but with competition born of a hatred that they have never surrendered into the flame, though they know not it is implanted within the subconscious. In an absence of the sense of justice, therefore, they serve in a sense of injustice that can never bring about harmony or the blending of all peoples in the service of Sanat Kumara.*

Therefore, I send forth a ray from my heart

*Sanat Kumara is an another name for the Ancient of Days (Dan. 7:9).

unto those who are the true shepherds of this people to elevate, to call you to action. And I summon Keepers of the Flame who recognize and sense the urgency in the heart of Saint Germain to go forth now—stumping in the name of the Mother, stumping in the name of the Lord of the World and in the name of the blessed Saviour Jesus to find the shepherds of this people, to isolate them by the sacred fire, to call them forth by love and offer to them the opportunity for the inheritance of the mantle of true shepherd.[25]

Reject Not the Mother of the Flame

Let none turn aside this opportunity to come under the tutelage of the Mother of the Flame[26] who is truly our representative in the Motherhood of all races under the blessed Omega and Mother Mary and of many hosts of the Lord. Therefore, let none take the teaching and separate themselves out from the teacher because the teacher does not, to outer appearances, qualify as being a part of the black people of this land.

No greater mistake could ever be made than for peoples to segment themselves according to outer judgment instead of the inner judgment of the heart. And yet I speak this because my children, many in number, have already rejected the Mother of the Flame because they have conceived of her as being what they call "white."

My beloved ones, this will not make for ascended master consciousness or evolution to these children of my heart. And therefore, prejudice runs strong in the hearts of people of all races, and it in itself is the outcropping of the projection of hatred of these fallen ones over thousands of years of manipulation of God's people to keep them divided. For every stream and lifewave manifesting as the varying races have somewhat to offer upon this planetary body.

And if there be those who say, "We will only take that which comes from our own people," they will be sadly denied the great blessings that come East and West through this River of Life[27] of the Mother that separates itself into divergent manifestations to show forth the glory, the beauty and the light of her infinite presence.

A Tide in the Affairs of the
Children of Afra

Thus, my beloved, let us realize that Saint Germain has said, even as he has told me this day, that there is a tide—a tide now in the affairs of the children of Afra—that must be taken, and taken in that moment when opportunity becomes a crystal light and a crystal sword.

Thus, there is fomenting in the fallen ones who have infiltrated the black movement the desire to instigate turmoil and riot and discontent, even as they have put upon them that belittlement and all of the evils of the drug culture and the withdrawal of the light of the culture of the Christ, the Buddha and the Mother.

The Fallen Ones Do Not Desire to See
the Children of Afra Rise

These fallen ones would not desire to see the children of Afra rise. And they have seen to it over several centuries in this nation and thousands of years in the homeland that they have been kept suppressed as well as oppressed—and my children have allowed it! Thus we look to the true shepherds to lead them to that higher consciousness. For I tell you, beloved ones, the fallen ones have determined to destroy the very heart and soul and purpose and mind of my children.

Though they know it not, the black people of America today are at the eternal Y, the place of choosing this day whom they will serve[28]—whether gains in the line of material comfort and increased well-being and higher-paying jobs or the real gain of the eternal light of Sonship and the path of immortality with all of its challenges as well as persecution as well as the great glory of the crucifixion itself.

My beloved ones, you cannot desire this world and the things that are in it and serve the god of mammon and arrive at that liberty that is the true liberty of Christ.[29] A materialistic consciousness is not always seen for what it is.

In this land of abundance and the great fulfillment of the message of the abundant life, it is natural for all people to expect and to live according to a higher standard of living. It is when this higher standard is able to obliterate from the soul and the heart the inner longing for the higher light and the higher way that it in itself becomes dangerous—not money but the love of money as the root of all evil,[30] as the messengers have told you. Therefore, it is the game of substitution, giving to my people a pacifier when truly the search for the light of the Spirit must prevail.

God Has Chosen This People

Therefore you must realize that though many are saying that the black people of America have been underprivileged and have not received the same opportunity as all, I would tell you that God has chosen this people as those who have become rich in Spirit by the deprivations in outer circumstances. Souls have made advancement on the path of sainthood and are reincarnating in this very hour, many among them who could, if they had the violet flame and this teaching, ascend in this life.

This opportunity for the path of initiation and sainthood has been abundantly given to those who were brought from the shores of Africa. Let them not, then, curse the fallen ones; for their very evil and the evil of the enemy itself has been the open door for the strength of character, for the light of Christ to evolve.

Therefore, you see that many who have had a life of ease and deference over these centuries have made little soul progress, whereas through the angels embodied among the black people, there is a spirit and a light, a power and a strength that can be galvanized and summoned and brought together now in such a conflagration of light, such a movement of liberation, as to make all previous efforts seem paltry before the great living Spirit of the Maha Chohan.*

The Mother of the Flame has held this image of the bursting forth of this pure stream of light and the real inner greatness of my people. This is why I have chosen to come. This is why I have been most grateful to answer the call of Saint Germain, because her heart has been one with my heart for centuries, and I can tell you that she knows, as I know, what is in the

*The Maha Chohan is an ascended master who conveys the flame of the Holy Spirit.

very inner being and inner causal body of these people who are the blacks of America. She has seen their coming and knows of that destiny. Therefore let those who have heard the call of Camelot realize what must be done.

The Fallen Ones Must Be Judged by Those Who Are of the Same Race and Group Karma

Yes, there are infiltrators within the race. Yes, there are tares sown among the wheat[31] as in all races, and they are there as destroyers to tear down. But God would build up. They are there to betray, but God would instill trust. They are there to perpetuate the lie, but Pallas Athena has brought the Truth.

These fallen ones know that when and where, in the very day and hour when the sons and daughters of Afra rise, that they shall be judged. For they must be judged by those who are of the same race and the same group karma.

These infiltrators, as there are the same infiltrators in all races, do embody from the astral plane out of the false hierarchy. They lay no claim to any race even as the fallen ones make no claim of loyalty as citizens of any nation. Therefore, they are the betrayers of the races. Therefore, they are the ones who keep back the children of the light and institute all sorts of social programmings—bussing for one—to destroy the light of the races. And they appear, wearing the garment of the particular race as it suits them, to push through legislation those programs that can only serve to further discredit, destroy and tear down the very integrity and individuality of the children of the light.

Thus, my beloved, I trust that all of you have long put behind you any sort of assessment of any of the peoples of earth saying that this or that group is intrinsically this or that. There is no group entirely good or entirely evil as the relative conditions of human consciousness go.

The Minorities in America Today

We see, then, looking at the minorities in America today, that some of these peoples have come from civilizations and societies where they have not had the opportunity to accelerate on the path of Christhood nor have they enjoyed the culture of the Divine Mother nor the fruits of a true understanding of the message of Jesus Christ. Therefore, whether they be from Vietnam or Cambodia, whether they come out of the East or from South America or even from the nations of Europe, many must have a greater opportunity to accelerate and come into the inheritance of the thirteen tribes of Israel, of the light and seed of Abraham.

Some among these minorities contain that seed as divine potential. Yet, it must flower, it must be nourished. They must be God-taught in the first principles of the Law, the Law that has been spoken by God from Sinai thousands of years ago and in ancient days by the very Ancient of Days himself.

Thus, opportunity is given and accelerated for the representatives of all peoples to now rise to the level of true shepherd, come into consonance with the plan divine of God, to cease from being separatists and going their separatist ways, to realize that this indeed is the logic of the fallen ones—to put off that yoke of bondage and enter into the confluence of the river of the Divine Mother, to come and accelerate, to come as chelas and thereby to receive the mantle by initiation whereby they may transfer the light of the messengers, of the ascended masters to the various peoples of their collective group karma and that which they represent.

Heaven Is Impartial

My beloved, I come with great joy, with great happiness, with great singing that there is a worldwide awakening among diverse peoples who have not thus far been offered the cup of Saint Germain. With those who are here and those who are in the field, it is possible for me to speak and to deliver the mantle and the dispensation of my causal body to you who earn it and would use it in the cause of freedom for all.

Heaven is impartial. We serve with all peoples. And we are dedicated to harmony, love and the divine plan for all to appear.

I trust, then, as I pray fervently in your behalf, that America may become the nation that will see the sons of Afra arise and take dominion and set the example of the culture of Afra blending with the culture of the New Age and of the Mother—to set the example and the Path and the open door of the ascension.

Long, long have I waited to see this day appear! Now, in this moment of opportunity and of its appearing, I salute you. I am with you and I say, Go to! I send you as the Lord has sent me.

And I will be with you! I will speak through you, and together we will turn back these fallen ones who have determined to destroy the cities of America and America as a whole by this division and by discontent and riot and all that shall not be, because we are *determined* that it shall not be and that they shall not pass!

Sons of flame, universally, hear my call! Hear my word!

We Are Committed to the Healing of All Schism in This and Every Nation

With me are companies of saints and angels. We are committed to the healing of all schism in this and every nation. We are committed to the true education of the heart, to the elevation of souls. We are committed to that healing light that will bind up those wounds that have never been healed.

Let them be *healed*, O God! Let them be *healed* by the light of the Woman descending now into the earth through these disciples of the light. Let them be healed, O God, and let this I AM Race arise in America in the true mantle of the Goddess of Liberty.

I am here! I have set my light to this God-determination. And those who are with me are determined that this earth shall not be split in two and that nations shall not be split in two and that individuals shall not be split in two by the ax forged of the hatred of the fallen ones.

We are determined that the greater love of light shall prevail. We are determined because you are here and because you have answered the call!

Now you seek to implement this desire of our hearts, and we are here to work through you. You need only to gather together, to counsel with the Lord and his hosts, and you will receive the answers and the divine direction that is needed.

Take courage, all. And take heart! There is yet an hour to give your life to the victory of Saint Germain.

Lo, I am his servant and his chela. Lo, I AM THAT I AM. ⚜

The Call of Camelot
July 5, 1980
Camelot
Los Angeles County, California

I Have Come to Call You Home—Call to Me

In 1996, Afra came once more with a message of hope for his people. He spoke of the need for a commitment to honor, of a path of dealing justly with God and with our brothers and sisters. He also called us to cut free souls caught in darkness. And whether this be violence, drugs, degradation or despair, the angels can come in answer to our prayers to rescue souls of light caught in these snares of death and hell.

I Have Come to Call You Home—Call to Me

Sons and daughters of Afra, sons and daughters of the God Star, I come to you in this hour. For in this hour, beloved, the fallen angels and aliens who have tormented you long, long, long ago and unto the present, they are off guard. They think they have you in their grips. Will you prove them wrong? [Audience responds: "Yes!"]

There is a time to sow and a time to reap.[32] There is a time to rise and there is a time to cleave unto the rocks and the caves. I tell you, beloved, all of the forces of evil in the earth, they think they have already done you in. Well, beloved, I have come to call you home—to call you home to the heart of the Mother of the World, who is indeed your true mother.

I call to you, then, to shed all those props

that you have set about yourselves. I say, obey the commandments of Moses. Obey the commandments and profound teachings of Jesus Christ. Do not think that because you have been mistreated so long that now, to even the score, you can take a little here and a little there. [If you do, you will] find yourselves once again enmeshed with the very fallen ones whom I have bound.

Be Honest in Your Heart and Mind

And therefore, I am the one who does say to you, liberate yourselves by taking unto your hearts the honor of God. When you carry that honor as the white lily of the fleur-de-lis, you shall know the white fire of your great teacher, El Morya. You shall understand that one does not cross the line into conceit and deceit if one expects to make his ascension in this life.

Therefore, be honest in your heart with your heart. Be honest in your mind with your mind. Know what you are, know what you are not. But know that always and always, through your Holy Christ Self and I AM Presence, you have the honor of God—you have it within you, and it shall grow and grow until it becomes that fiery steel pillar.

None can keep you from entering the gates of heaven. But you must understand that there is no time to be concerned with getting even. One never knows, beloved, what is the karmic cause of one's condition. Have you come as angels of light to embody now among the sons and daughters of Afra? Have you come because you had very good karma or perhaps very bad karma? It is not necessary to know.

But one must know that this day, at this point in time and space before this altar, you will make your commitment to Sanat Kumara and you will keep it. And you will train your children in the way that they must go. And that way is the way of impeccability—impeccability of conscience, of profound love, and such a sword, such a steely white fire, to *purge* elements that no one else may see in yourself except you and God. Yet, you are transparent to all angels.

The Seven Archangels Are Your Champions

Therefore, beloved, I point out to you that the seven archangels are your champions. And so long as you keep the honor flame with them, with God, with your I AM Presence, they are at your side instantaneously. There is no end to the numbers of angels connected to this planetary home and beyond.

And so, beloved, walk upright before your God. I speak of honor, because without honor, my plan for you will fail. You must have that cosmic honor flame and never cross the line, embracing conceit and deceit as though they were [legitimate] choices to bypass [laws that are] not the laws of man but the laws of God that are translated to those who would walk this path.

There is nothing that you want that you cannot have if you walk the straight and narrow way. I am not accusing you of not walking this way. But I say for this wise, beloved: I have summoned many angels. They have come. The Mother of the Flame is determined to sponsor you. So you see, beloved, we give from our causal bodies, as do many of the ascended masters. Therefore we must reiterate the principles, the first principles, beloved. And if you fail them not and walk that path, no matter what, and you are in the righteousness of God, you shall be as I AM one day. You shall know me as Afra. You shall move with me as an ascended master.

And what shall the color of your skin be? It does not matter. I do not know. And I am not concerned. And you ought not to be concerned either.

I Am Not Leaving This Nation or This Planet

I call upon you, then, you who have developed your heart flames, you who have such a love for the ascended masters, you who have borne burdens for your people. I am here. I am not leaving this nation or this planet. There is an open door, beloved. The astrology is written in the skies, and it is written in your inward parts: this is the hour of the liberation of the sons and daughters of Afra. And I tell you, the contribution of your people, our people, shall be one that shall cover the earth.

And what we find, beloved, as many of you have descended as angels, angels to move midst my people, so you have gained a tremendous love in your beings. You move with [the archangels] Chamuel and Charity. You are giving of love and giving and giving of self again and again. Therefore millions of you, beloved, are walking about as comforting angels, not only to one people but to all people.

I say, then, it is imperative that your numbers increase—not that we depend upon numbers, beloved, but that many must know the glory of the Lord so that when the glory of the Lord comes upon you and upon this people throughout the earth, you shall be their teachers. You shall move with Kuthumi. You shall move with Jesus. And you shall give to them a profound understanding of the Law so that they will not go out of the way and create karma and go down into despair again and again until they cry out—yet their cry is not heard, for they have descended so far into the depths of the astral plane that the ascended masters do not descend to that level.

Therefore, it is as though you will have a perpetual wake for the rest of your lives, calling for the cutting free of these magnificent souls who have been entrapped in the lower levels of the astral plane by the fallen angels and those aliens. These souls, beloved, have yet to have their day.

We Must Make Our Mark

Your souls, our souls, we must make our mark in such a way as to put to shame those who do not meet our standards. See and understand this. Let people look at your countenance and see the shining of your aura. Let them say, "I would be like this one. I would be a brother to all. I would be a sister to all. I would comfort. I would console. I would seek the Holy Spirit. I would seek the Prince of Peace. I must walk in the shadow of the Almighty. For this is my day, this is my hour that I shall lead my people to the throne of glory."

O blessed ones, I cast out now *greed*—greed in the very core of this people. Be stripped, then, of that desire for name and fame and money. It will kill you. It will surely kill the body as well as the soul. This is the straying on the lines of the clock of indulgence, extreme indulgence—a compensation. What for? For having gone through long travail, long travail through many aeons.

Beloved hearts, this is the Path. I say to you, walk ye in it. And any time you feel the light of your heart descend below that heart chakra, know that you are being sucked down into vials of depression—depression, despair that takes you down, down, down. And how will you climb back up that spiral staircase if you have not the Kundalini fire on the altar of the spine itself?

The Archangels Require Your Prayers

Yes, beloved ones, many souls are being lost today. And they are being lost because the archangels or angels require your prayers that they might descend into death and hell and cut free those souls who have been tormented, who have been bruised, who have been spat upon, who have been treated not even as human beings.

All this is as though you are seeing a motion

picture on the screen as you see, ages past, how you have reincarnated in Egypt, in this land, in the next land, how you have risen, how you have fallen, how some of you have almost reached the point of your ascension so many times and yet were wooed away by clever serpents in the Garden of Eden.

Oh, yes, beloved, be smart, because you *are* smart. You are very smart. You are astute. You read people. You read this messenger. I need not tell you anything about her, because you know it. And that is why you are here. You have a sixth sense about many things. But what will give you the empowerment is your moving with the angels and setting an example of turning the other cheek—even if that cheek has been turned over and over again. Never stop!

It Does Not Matter What Body We Wear

Is it somehow beneath us to be humble? No. We are humble because we have seen the majesty of our God, and we know that in the last day and the last trump our God shall raise us into the victory of our ascension. And we shall see ourselves in the glory of who we are as angels, as we were when God created us.

So it does not matter what body we wear. Our body is like a uniform. We come to deal with certain souls that are a part of us, and we are a part of them, and we self-identify as one. This is the great mystery of life, beloved, a profound mystery.

I Pledge to You My Life, My Love

I, then, pledge to you my life, my love. I stand with the Holy Spirit. And I stand through that Spirit to convey to you everything you need—everything you need, I have said, and remember it—everything you need to fulfill your mission, to conquer the evil forces in this earth, to turn around this enslavement of some people, beautiful people, beautiful children of the Mother of the World.

I tell you, this is a literal statement. You are standing before your Mother. And this Mother will never ever let you go.

Know this, beloved: This is the hour when your Holy Christ Self will release to you from your causal bodies a quotient of energy sufficient to resolve this issue of race, when race should never have been an issue *ever* upon this earth.

O beloved, I take from my causal body and many others with me. We are counting upon you to embrace one another, to embrace the Mother, the true Mother who loves you, and to recognize that when you come together with that intense union, you will be a fireball in the planet. And you will gather more unto yourselves of the greatest of lightbearers—those of tremendous education, those of scientific understanding, those who are capable in government, in education, and so on and so on.

Yes, beloved: The timetable is now. This is the moment; this is the open door. Take it. Open it. Seize it. Sacrifice. Give service. Surrender. And come to that point where you know that nothing, *nothing* can deter you from your victory.

Sons and daughters of Afra, are you with me? [Audience responds: "Yes!"]

So let it be. The empowerment shall be unto you through my causal body and through the causal body of Lanello and the Mother of the Flame. Call upon us, for you must make the call. And do not let one moment of your life any longer contain even a thimbleful of discouragement. This is your hour and the power of light! As Jesus said to the devil, "This is your hour, and the power of darkness,"[33] so the tables are turned. They are on the run. Beware of spacecraft—they are making their last-ditch attempt to move against not only yourselves but all people of this earth.

A Special Blessing

I now come with a special blessing. And as you might suspect, the blessing I bring is the cosmic honor code. And that code is a circle of fire. I seal it upon you. And if you are true to yourselves, you will never again be able to violate the laws of God. And that, beloved, shall be the beginning of our victory.

I want you to know that I am a strategist. You ought to meet and plan your strategies for your nation, for this nation, for your state, for your city. Strategize, beloved. For it shall take much ingenuity and profound prayer to make this happen in this timetable.

Therefore, my blessing to you is a fiery coin the size of a dollar. And that coin has such fire in it that you can hardly look upon it. Seal it over your heart chakra. Engraven upon this coin is "I shall be true to myself and to my God."

In the name of the Father, the Son, the Holy Spirit and the Divine Mother, I seal you in the path of everlasting life. If you do not attain it, beloved, it will not be because I did not try with the greatest of my fervor of being to accomplish this with you and through you. Call to me. I am just a knock away.

Nothing Can Stop Us When We Are One

My beloved, I am grateful beyond words to all people who have come to establish this place in the wilderness, protected by millions of acres of national park, Forest Service land, and so forth. Beloved ones, it is indeed a great retreat.[34]

I am grateful, then, for all that has gone before since the beginning of The Summit Lighthouse, that those who were its founders and those who have pressed on and many who have made their ascension were true to their calling and, therefore, this day can welcome you and rejoice that in the fruit of their labors they have been able to give you the gift of themselves.

Truly, I love you. I have loved you from the beginning. I shall love you unto the ending. And I shall never leave you unless you command me to be gone. And even then, I will argue with you. [laughter]

With my love, go forth. Nothing can stop us when we are one, when we are our brothers' keepers, our sisters' keepers.

In the joy of the Lord, I bless you now with that sealing. ✤

A World Convocation of Spiritual Seekers
June 27, 1996
The Royal Teton Ranch
Park County, Montana

If You Would Attain
Union with God, Bond
to the Lord Krishna

In his final message, Afra brings us to Krishna, great saint of the East. Krishna came to India long ages before the time of Jesus, yet he came to bear witness to that same light, the Christ that "before Abraham was, I AM." Many myths and legends have grown up around Krishna, yet we can know him today as he is—a great light and an open door to the Universal Presence of the Christ.

If You Would Attain Union with God, Bond to the Lord Krishna

Lo! I AM Afra, and I manifest my presence here. And to every heart on earth I send forth needlelike rays that there might be perception, manifestation and the internalization of the white fire of God within all.

All are of the white fire of God. All races in the earth receive that white fire from the Great Central Sun in the core of their being. This fire is sent forth to gather the nations, to raise up the children of Afra, to raise up those who have not been raised up because of their absence of self-worth and a nonacknowledgment of the threefold flame that burns upon the altar of their hearts.

Today I go before the Lord Morya El to clear the way for his coming, for this is indeed his day. Will you not stand in his honor? [Audience rises.] Out of the sun of Aries does this beloved ascended master come to us. And out of that sun comes the majesty of God-control whereby all things come into union and the living presence of Alpha and Omega draweth nigh.

Know Your Mentor as Your Holy Christ

Contemplate now the presence of your Holy Christ Self. O ye sons and daughters of Afra, I counsel you to go to the secret chamber of your heart and to know your mentor as your own beloved Holy Christ Self. Only thus shall you become one with that Holy Christ Self and ultimately attain union with God through the ascension.

This is so of all peoples in the earth. Therefore, let none of the billions of souls on planet Earth deny the living presence of the entire Spirit of the Great White Brotherhood,*

---

*The Great White Brotherhood is a spiritual order of saints and adepts of every race, culture and religion. These masters have transcended the cycles of karma and rebirth and reunited with the Spirit of the living God. The word "white" refers to the aura or halo of white light that surrounds them.

regardless of the background of their evolution.

This is the hour when all who are on earth must understand that their branches have intertwined and been a part of each other for aeons. Therefore, earth is a melting pot, and we would see the dross skimmed off the top. We would see the fire descend and the gold of God consciousness be all-pervasive that everyone might walk in the dignity of the golden aura of the Buddhic presence and golden aura of the Lord Krishna.

Bond to the Lord Krishna

Now at this juncture in my delivery, I ask you to sing to the Lord Krishna, for his universal presence is manifest in each one of your hearts. I am calling home those who are of the evolutions of Afra and those of every race and nation. Therefore, in the depths of your soul reach out to this great one.

[Audience sings devotional songs to Krishna.]

Beloved hearts, I am sent by Lord Krishna. He does come as the court of last resort for many, not only for the sons and daughters of Afra but also for all throughout the earth who have not understood how lethal are what you have called the Martian A's,[35] especially the manifestation of anger.

Some chelas who have passed through this organization have not understood the necessity of God-control, and their threefold flame has been snuffed out. This is indeed a tragedy.

Therefore, the Lord Krishna asked that you might sing this bhajan to him that he might reach down into the hearts of all on earth who are associated with the Great White Brotherhood. This is the time, this is the place. This is the moment to reverse the course of negation that, if left to itself, will ultimately negate the soul in those who have not applied themselves to the highest manifestation of the Lord God and the Lord

Renewed Opportunity

Therefore, beloved, know all aspects of the Lord Krishna's life. Recite the mantras. Know that you play a role in the life cycles of Krishna from the time of his birth to this hour.

We give to all renewed opportunity. For

many have been duped and led astray by fallen angels. Others have taken upon themselves the anger of the fallen angels when they themselves did not initially have that anger.

The hour is come when forgiveness can be given to those who seemingly know not what they do, although their souls know what they do.[36] Beyond this, beloved, understand that if you allow yourselves to get out of alignment with the harmony of God and therefore begin to lose increments of the threefold flame, the inner soul and the Atman, you may have to return at a future time beyond this dispensation of the open door and take a chance that once again the flame of mercy will be placed upon you.

Therefore, call upon the law of forgiveness. Report to Lord Krishna. Write letters to him and then burn them as an act of profound devotion and an imploring to his heart. Neglect not the Krishna mantras as you move from place to place. For in these mantras you shall find life, liberation and tremendous illumination.

You Must Achieve Soul Resolution

This is a serious moment in the history of the lightbearers. The messengers have preached to you for many years. The hour has come when the Lords of Karma must say: We draw the line. We move into the age of Aquarius. We cannot carry with us those who do not have resolution in their souls, in their hearts.

May each one ponder the dilemma of his future. Go to the heart of Sanat Kumara, Lord Gautama and Lord Jesus Christ to make your peace, through the law of forgiveness, with all whom you have wronged. This do, beloved, and know your freedom day by day.

Some have snuffed out the flame of the Atman.* They are not even aware that the process has taken place, so enmired are they in the human consciousness. Let this not be the fate of our best servants or the least of the brethren.

*The indwelling Presence of God.

Give Lord Krishna's Mantras to Fan the Threefold Flame

Now receive Lord Krishna. And if you would fan your threefold flame, remember the mantras. And when you are beset by anger, remember to seal your lips. Yes, seal the place where evil dwells and seek your resolution in God.

Many of you have served the Great White Brotherhood in this activity for decades, and you have served in similar activities in recent lifetimes. You have had plenty of opportunity to fulfill your mission in this life. Therefore, for each the bell shall toll. And when it tolls, beloved, it will be the sign of your final opportunity to make resolution and peace with your inner being and the Elohim of God.

Rescue My Sons and Daughters!

I AM Afra. I have come with this message for all peoples. But I now turn specifically to my people throughout the world and I say: Many of you are angels of light who have moved through the nations, who have cut free the sons and daughters of Afra. But many others came to

143

earth after you. These are the corrupt ones and the fallen angels who have tormented you and your children, who have tormented fathers who then leave, forcing the mother to take full responsibility for the family.

Blessed ones, many sons and daughters of Afra are vulnerable because many of them have snuffed out their threefold flames for the sheer hopelessness of their lives. And this is easily done through misuses of the sacred fire in any of the chakras.

I call to all sons and daughters of Afra and those moving with you to rescue your people. I call upon you and I say: Use the dynamic decrees given to you by the messengers and the ascended masters. Call for the judgment of the fallen angels. Call for them to be bound and removed from the earth and taken to the Court of the Sacred Fire on the God Star, Sirius, where they will stand trial and be brought to judgment.[37]

Blessed ones, this is the call of the hour. Purge your people and the people of earth. Let the shining ones rise to the top, and let the others be bound. Beware of the forces of Antichrist throughout the earth, and be one in heart, soul and mind.

Invite Krishna to Live in the Secret Chamber of Your Heart

Allow Krishna to enter your temple and through his love comfort one another, love one another, bond with one another. And the flowering of your soul, your heart, your mind and your chakras shall show to the world and a cosmos what can be the full beauty of the manifestation of the Lord Krishna when the individual disciple welcomes him into his temple.

This do, beloved. Invite Krishna to live in the secret chamber of your heart, in the Atman, and chant the Krishna mantra. For thereby those who may have faltered, gone astray or lost their light might be pulled back by Krishna's mighty power.

I, then, bow to the light within you. And I say to all who are my sons and daughters: Beware. Be not led astray. Come into communion with the Holy Spirit. Mothers, fathers, children, recognize the tremendous light in your beings. Go after the light and expand it. For you can make your ascension in this life if you will follow this path and this teaching. ⚜

Easter Retreat 1997
April 4, 1997
The Royal Teton Ranch
Park County, Montana

The Chart of Your
Divine Self

The Chart of Your Divine Self is a portrait of
you and of the God within you. It is a dia-
gram of you and your potential to become who
you really are. It is an outline of your spiritual
anatomy.

The upper figure is your "I AM Presence,"
the Presence of God that is individualized in
each one of us. It is your personalized "I AM
THAT I AM." Your I AM Presence is surrounded
by seven concentric spheres of spiritual energy
that make up what is called your "Causal Body."
The spheres of pulsating energy contain the
record of the good works you have performed
since your very first incarnation on earth. They
are like your cosmic bank account.

The middle figure in the Chart represents

the "Holy Christ Self," who is also called the Higher Self. You can think of your Holy Christ Self as your chief guardian angel and dearest friend, your inner teacher and voice of conscience. Just as the I AM Presence is the presence of God that is individualized for each of us, so the Holy Christ Self is the presence of the Universal Christ that is individualized for each of us. "The Christ" is actually a title given to those who have attained oneness with their Higher Self, or Christ Self. That's why Jesus was called "Jesus, the Christ."

The shaft of white light descending from the I AM Presence through the Holy Christ Self to the lower figure in the Chart is the crystal cord (sometimes called the silver cord). It is the "umbilical cord," the lifeline, that ties you to Spirit.

Your crystal cord also nourishes that special, radiant flame of God in the secret chamber of your heart. It is called the threefold flame, or divine spark, because it is literally a spark of sacred fire that God has transmitted from his heart to yours. This flame is called "threefold" because it includes the primary attributes of Spirit—power, wisdom and love.

The lower figure in the Chart of Your Divine Self represents you on the spiritual path, surrounded by the violet flame and the protective white light of God. The soul is the living potential of God—the part of you that is mortal but that can become immortal.

The purpose of your soul's evolution is to grow in self-mastery, balance your karma and fulfill your mission on earth so that you can return to the spiritual dimensions that are your real home. When your soul at last takes flight and ascends back to God and the heaven-world, you will become an ascended master, free from the rounds of karma and rebirth. The energy of the violet flame can help you reach that goal more quickly. ⚜

Notes

NOTES TO SECTION I
Dictations by Afra referenced in these notes are published in full in section III.

1. Gen. 4:8–9.

2. Excerpted and adapted by Elizabeth Clare Prophet from a dictation by Afra delivered September 18.

3. Afra, June 27, 1996.

4. Excerpted and adapted by Elizabeth Clare Prophet from a dictation by Afra, July 5, 1980.

5. Ibid.

6. Elizabeth Clare Prophet, *Inner Perspectives* (Corwin Springs, Mont.: The Summit Lighthouse Library, 2001), p. 192.

7. Matt. 13:38–39.

8. Mark L. Prophet and Elizabeth Clare Prophet, *Climb the Highest Mountain: The Path of the Higher Self* (Corwin Springs, Mont.: Summit University Press, 1986), pp. 109–10.

9. All that transpires in an individual's world and all events in the physical universe are recorded in an

etheric substance and dimension known as akasha (Sanskrit, "from the root"). Akasha is primary substance, the subtlest, ethereal essence, which fills the whole of space; "etheric" energy vibrating at a certain frequency so as to absorb, or record, all of the impressions of life.

10. *Climb the Highest Mountain: The Path of the Higher Self,* p. 110.

11. Kuthumi, July 21, 1972.

12. Mark 3:35.

13. Matt. 25:40.

14. Luke 19:26.

NOTES TO SECTION II

1. Rom. 12:19.

2. John 5:14.

3. Luke 23:34.

4. Robin Casarjian, *Forgiveness: A Bold Choice for a Peaceful Heart* (New York: Bantam Books, 1992), p. 236.

5. Matt. 6:12.

6. Jer. 31:34.

7. John 5:17.

8. Casarjian, *Forgiveness: A Bold Choice for a Peaceful Heart,* p. 214.

NOTES TO SECTION III

1. John 13:16; 15:20.

2. John 1:9.

3. Elizabeth Clare Prophet, *The Astrology of the Four Horsemen* (Corwin Springs, Mont.: Summit University Press, 1991), pp. 52–53.

4. Ibid, p. 58.

5. During the long winter at Valley Forge, Micah, the Angel of Unity, appeared to George Washington in a vision of three great perils that would come upon the nation—the Revolutionary War, the War between the States, and a third world conflict. According to Anthony Sherman's account of this vision, Washington related that he was shown the inhabitants of America "in battle array against each other. As I continued looking I saw a bright angel, on whose brow rested a crown of light, on which was traced the word 'Union,' bearing the American flag which he placed between the divided nation, and said, 'Remember ye are brethren.' Instantly, the inhabitants, casting from them their weapons, became friends once more and united around the National Standard." (*Saint Germain On Alchemy* [Corwin Springs, Mont.: Summit University Press, 1993], pp. 142–51.)

6. Henry Wadsworth Longfellow, *The Song of Hiawatha,* Part 1: "The Peace Pipe."

7. *E pluribus unum* (Latin, "one out of many"): the original motto adopted for the Great Seal of the United States. It refers to the American determination to form a unified nation from people of

diverse beliefs and backgrounds.

8. Rev. 1:8; 21:6; 22:13.

9. Dan. 7:9, 13, 22.

10. Matt. 23:37; Luke 13:34.

11. Matt. 28:18.

12. Matt. 4:9; Luke 4:6, 7.

13. Matt. 26:39; Mark 14:36; Luke 22:42.

14. Rev. 17:1; 19:20; 20:1–3.

15. 1 Kings 4:25; Mic. 4:4; Zech. 3:10.

16. Jer. 31:33.

17. Gen. 4:4.

18. Josh. 24:15.

19. Eph. 2:20.

20. Prov. 29:18.

21. Gen. 3:4.

22. Dan. 12:2; Rev. 2:11; 20:6, 14; 21:8.

23. Portia, "A Council of the Woman Clothed with the Sun: Delivering a Path for the Liberation of Woman through Mighty Cosmos' Five Secret Rays," *Pearls of Wisdom,* vol. 23, no. 29, July 20, 1980.

24. Luke 3:1–18.

25. Jer. 23:1–4; John 10:1–18.

26. The Mother of the Flame is an office and a mantle occupied by Elizabeth Clare Prophet.

27. Rev. 22:1.

28. Josh. 24:15.

29. Matt. 6:24; Luke 16:9–13.

30. 1 Tim. 6:10.

31. Matt. 13:24–30, 36–43.

32. Eccles. 3:2.

33. Luke 22:53.

34. This dictation was delivered at the Royal Teton Ranch, international headquarters of The Summit Lighthouse. The ranch is situated in North America's Rocky Mountains, on the northern border of Yellowstone National Park.

35. Long ago, the evolutions of Mars took the pure white light of the Mother and perverted it in war and misuses of the sacred fire. These misqualifications can manifest through any of the chakras but specifically relate to the misuse of the Mother light in the base-of-the-spine chakra. They include: aggression, anger, arrogance, argumentation, accusation, agitation, apathy, atheism, annihilation, aggravation, annoyance, aggressive mental suggestion; criticism, condemnation and judgment. The fact that so many of these misqualifications begin with the letter A indicates that they are also a perversion of the light of the Father, Alpha.

36. Luke 23:34.

37. John the Evangelist's vision of this judgment is recorded in Revelation chapter 20.

A Note from the Editors

The teachings in this book are compiled from the lectures, dictations, books and sermons of Elizabeth Clare Prophet. They include the discourses given by the master Afra through his messenger. The teaching and concepts belong to her. We have simply woven the threads and connected the thoughts to make the whole.

The Editors of The Summit Lighthouse Library

Elizabeth Clare Prophet, A Servant of the Light

*E*lizabeth Clare Prophet is a servant of the light in all people. She once described her unique role as messenger for the masters of light, as follows:

"The ascended masters present a path and a teaching whereby every individual on earth can find his way back to God. I do not claim to be a master but only their instrument. Nor do I claim to be perfect in my human self. I am the servant of the light in all students of the ascended masters and in all people.

"My books and writings are intended to give people the opportunity to know the truth that can make them free—so they can find God without me. My goal is to take true seekers, in the tradition of the masters of the Far East, as far as they can go and need to go to meet their true teachers face-to-face."

Many of Elizabeth Clare Prophet's books contain the enlightened teachings and dictations from these beings of light.

Other books by
Elizabeth Clare Prophet

The Path of Brotherhood
Wanting to Be Born
Violet Flame to Heal Body, Mind and Soul
The Creative Power of Sound
Saint Germain On Alchemy
Fallen Angels and the Origins of Evil
The Lost Years of Jesus
The Lost Teachings of Jesus

For More Information

For more information about The Summit Lighthouse Library, to place an order or to receive a free catalog of our books and products, please contact us at:

The Summit lighthouse Library
PO Box 5000
Corwin Springs, MT 59030-5000, USA
Tel: 1-800-245-5445 or 406-848-9500
Fax: 1-800-221-8307 or 406-848-9555
www.summituniversitypress.com
info@summituniversitypress.com